THE 100 BEST
WAYS TO
MEET PEOPLE

QUANTITY SALES

Most Dell books are available at special quantity discounts when purchased in bulk by corporations, organizations, or groups. Special imprints, messages, and excerpts can be produced to meet your needs. For more information, write to: Dell Publishing, 1540 Broadway, New York, NY 10036. Attention: Director, Special Markets.

INDIVIDUAL SALES

Are there any Dell books you want but cannot find in your local stores? If so, you can order them directly from us. You can get any Dell book currently in print. For a complete up-to-date listing of our books and information on how to order, write to: Dell Readers Service, Box DR, 1540 Broadway, New York, NY 10036.

THE 100 BEST WAYS TO MEET PEOPLE

*Simple Truths, Surprising Insights
into What Keeps People Apart,
and What Gets People Together*

Ben White

A Dell Book

Published by
Dell Publishing
a division of
Bantam Doubleday Dell Publishing Group, Inc.
1540 Broadway
New York, New York 10036

ISBN: 0-440-22572-8

Printed in the United States of America

Published simultaneously in Canada

February 1998

10 9 8 7 6 5 4 3 2 1

OPM

Dedicated to every person who ever stood across a crowded room from someone who dazzled and intimidated them and, with heart pounding and palms sweating, crossed that immeasurable distance and said hello.

As smart as you are, as savvy as you may be, it seems that meeting people—or at least meeting the *right* person these days—is up there next to winning the lottery.

At least that seems true for a large and growing number of single people, even many who are attractive and successful, and particularly for those whose odometers have reached thirty, thirty-five, and beyond.

It's true even here in San Francisco's somewhat famous Marina District, fifteen or twenty square blocks of practically nothing but single people of all ages. Who'd imagine that *The 100 Best Ways to Meet People*, which had its origins in my column in the *Marina Times*, would be requested so often and tie up its staff so much, that my editor admonished me never to even mention it in my column again?

The demand surprised them and me. But it shouldn't have. Paradise this may be; but we're strangers in paradise.

"Everybody's looking," says Nancy, an intelligent and attractive redheaded divorcée. But if that's true, *where'd everybody go*? Where—and how—do you find a credible candidate for a relationship?

What do you do after you've gone out once too often to trendy nightspots, had the same vacuous conversations you've had a thousand times before, seen few or no people who interested you or were approachable, and come home with nothing but tired feet and depleted resources?

Most single people agree it's just plain hard to meet other single people.

"Have you heard of that dating service called Great Expectations?" says Cindy, an attractive forty-something single. "Well, I have *no* expectations!"

"We meet, but we don't *connect*," says Mark, a writer in his thirties. "It's like we're in separate spheres."

"He was gorgeous," said a charming blonde named Christy after a workout at the San Francisco Bay Club. "And every time he looked at me, I looked away."

One attractive woman I know tried to get the attention of a guy she liked while she was waiting at a deli counter. "I just don't get it," she said. "I thought I was sending every signal I could. What did I have to do to get his attention, set myself on flames?"

Here in the Marina and environs, on a typical Saturday there are literally thousands of singles simply walking, jogging, or biking down the street. Yet what guy or gal has the chutzpah to approach an absolute stranger? (Have you ever wondered why most of us can't? What inhibits us? What is it about our culture, our instincts, our fears, that so narrowly prescribes when and where it's okay to relax, smile, and say hello?)

Of course, some people don't try to meet people. Some even have philosophical reasons for their inaction. How often have you heard, "Just when you least expect it, you find it." Or "It'll happen if it's meant to be!"

Splendid! That's just what you've been waiting to hear. Do you really believe there will be divine intervention in your life all of a sudden? That heaven itself is troubled because you don't have a date Saturday night? This would be an even shorter book if I believed that. I'd simply have one suggestion: Do nothing! (Seriously, can you think of any endeavor in life in which you can produce results by doing nothing?)

Then there are the people who don't meet people because they claim their careers or avocations demand everything from them. There are the procrastinators who plan to think about it tomorrow. There are people who simply don't make meeting people a priority. The list is exhaustive: We're too busy, too tired, too frazzled, too proud, too inhibited.

Too bad. It doesn't matter why you aren't meeting people; the results are the same: one more rented movie, a pizza, and cold sheets.

Here's the bottom line: You can wait around for fate to intervene. Or you can try to do something about the situation.

If you choose the latter, I am happy to share such truths as I possess, gleaned from my own experience and hundreds of interviews and conversations with both single people and couples.

Hint. There are two key ways to meet people:

1. Change your attitude. Stop wringing your hands about the unfairness of it all, stop looking backward, and stop putting everything off until tomorrow.

2. Change your actions (or inactions). Your present course isn't getting you where you want to go—right?—or you wouldn't be reading this.

Someone once said that 80 percent of success is just showing up. Simple; start showing up!

I confess that few of my one hundred ways to meet people are revolutionary. You will not faint dead away from the shock of the unexpected, or be swept away by my profundity. (Well, maybe occasionally.)

You have already done many of these things, and few will lead you directly to the person of your dreams. You will kiss a lot of frogs without finding a prince. I personally don't, can't, or won't do some of these things.

But if you buy into the attitude, you can't help but dramatically increase your odds. You'll find that it becomes easier and easier to meet people, that *just doing it* defuses your anxieties and bolsters your confidence.

And all you have to do to get started is to walk out your front door.

Just remember through it all that you have nothing to lose and so much to gain: from developing an ever-widening circle of friends, to connecting at last with a soulmate who has probably been looking for you. And what a joyful, thrilling, unending discovery that can be.

1. *Smile.*

2. Just say hello;
never use a "line" to meet anyone.

3. Tolerate lines.

4. Go "hunting" with a friend
of the *opposite* sex.

Couples can meet people more easily
than singles. Don't worry about the
initial impression that you're a
pair; your stock actually goes up.
Your friend can easily open a
conversation when you can't:
"Where'd you get those earrings?"
"Have you heard the score?"

5. Never do anything at home
that you can do in a park.

6. Host a party in the next thirty days.

7. When you give a party,
ask everyone to invite at least one person
who's outside your group.

10. *Accept rejection as a cost
of doing business.*

12. Get up the nerve to ask.

13. *Recognize that the person approaching you had to get up the nerve to ask.*

14. *Don't judge at a glance.*

15. Start more sentences with "You."
End more sentences with question marks.

When you meet people, do you
commence an information dump about
yourself? Or do you draw them out
instead? People try so hard to develop
lines and acts, when they can usually get
a lot farther by simply asking real
questions and exhibiting genuine interest
in other people. As an experiment, one
person I know "worked a room" and
made a point of only asking questions,
volunteering as little as possible about
himself. After he'd left the room, one
person after another commented about
how fascinating they thought he was;
yet he'd said practically nothing.

16. Fix people up.

Be less critical than you are about matchmaking. Don't wait till you've got two people who are just perfect for each other. Fix up any people who have the remotest chance of working. I know a number of couples I'd never have thought to pair up.

17. Be fixed up.

18. Lighten up.

19. Join a health club, *and get in shape.*

This one's a no-brainer. You probably belong to a health club already, but do you use it? Lots can change along with your body. Your endorphins kick in, and it actually gets easier and more fun. So go, and praise yourself every moment that you work out. You'll look better, you'll feel better, you'll *be* better, and you'll be in better shape physically and spiritually to meet somebody, in or out of the club.

20. Don't apply the "Three Strikes and You're Out" rule to dating.

You may be in such a hurry to meet the right person that you're discarding one right person after another. There seems to be an unwritten rule that if there aren't fireworks by date three or sooner, it's history. But many couples say one or both of them weren't swept away right away. (Harry and Sally didn't even *like* each other when they met.) And some affairs that start incandescently are often, as Cole Porter wrote, "too hot not to cool down." The Oakland Fire ignited from infinitesimal sparks—and the day after everyone thought it was out.

22. Kick your ass out of bed.

23. Call her.

You obtained her number or her extension at work, but now the phone seems as frightening as a time bomb. You just know she's dating someone, she's unattainable, she thinks you're a geek. *Pick up the phone and dial.* Chances are you'll just get her answering machine anyway. (Sometimes that's a great way to state your case, even ask her out, all electronically.) This also applies to phone numbers you've procrastinated about, and to women who said no six months ago. Remember point #10.

24. Call him.

It's the nineties.

25. Get "call waiting."

26. Call everybody you haven't spoken with for six months or longer.

People who aren't part of your daily life may change your life one day, if you simply keep in touch. Just pick up the phone and *be interested* in acquaintances, old friends, exes (unless you really can't stand them), business contacts, relatives, *everybody*. I've yet to receive anything but a positive response. In fact, at various times I've personally gotten a new job, a new relationship, and rekindled a romance I'd thought long gone—all from keeping in touch with people I already knew.

27. Dress for access.

This isn't an easy call; everyone's different, and there are varying dress codes among different ages, occupations, and occasions. Overdressing or the look of excessive affluence may actually be a barrier, especially for women; less so for men. Guys often underdress. Many single women wear rings that are mistaken for wedding bands. When in doubt, keep things subtle and avoid extremes. *You* should stand out, not your fluorescent pink blouse or zany tie. Men, ask trusted *women* friends for an honest wardrobe assessment. Women, ask *male* friends.

28. Go dancing!

29. Be a tourist in your own town.

30. Expand your territory.

Jump on cable cars, buses, or trains and
get off at new stops. Go shopping in
different grocery stores, hardware stores,
plant shops, and other places than your
usual ones. Drive to outlying
communities or towns and explore. Hop
on an airplane and go anywhere you can
afford for a day, an evening, a weekend,
or longer.

31. Read neighborhood newspapers.

32. Get your Sunday newspaper
on Saturday—for the calendar of events.

33. Go to exhibits, shows, and conventions.

You don't really have to be in the business involved, just interested. Ask your local convention centers to mail you their annual calendar. It may surprise you how many varieties of events never make the newspaper, because they're theoretically just for the trade (sporting equipment, furniture, art deco, gifts, kitchen and bath . . .).

35. Get a pet with lots of character
and hang out together.

36. Make more friends of the same sex.

37. Make more friends of the opposite sex.

38. Try the personals.

This isn't for everyone. But many people
don't realize that if you are the *writer*,
you're in absolute control of this
procedure. You receive messages on a
distant voice-mail system, and you decide
who, how, and if you reply. Request that
callers leave a voice-mail message and/or
send a letter, photo, résumé, or anything
else you wish to the box number you're
assigned. If you're the caller, you
sacrifice control, which carries obvious
risks. Especially if you're a woman,
consider leaving a message that describes
you without pinpointing you, and
requests a letter, bio, photo, etc. Then
decide if you wish to call.

40. Drop your preconceived notions.

It's natural to be specific about what
you're looking for, and what you're not,
especially the longer you've been at it.
But opening up to different kinds of
people and ideas may lead you to
unexpectedly fortuitous opportunities
and choices. (Consider people you've
known who have passed judgment on *you*
based on hasty, incomplete, or inaccurate
information, or simply by being closed
minded.) Try to set aside the things your
parents told you, peer pressures,
stereotypes, appearances, and your other
assumptions. You may be surprised at the
depth, beauty, and potential of many
people when you look at them with fresh
eyes and an open mind.

42. Learn to draw, paint, sculpt,
write, or play.

43. Go out with friends more often.

44. *Go out alone more often.*

45. Hang out in coffeehouses
instead of bars.

46. Walk, jog, and bicycle for recreation and *transportation* whenever you can.

47. Never miss a party of any kind
unless you have a temperature of 104 or over.

48. Put *her* behind you.

49. Put *him* behind you.

50. Don't go looking for someone you lost
in somebody else.

51. *Stay friends with your exes.*

My parents dated, then married other people, and married each other years later.

52. Volunteer.

Volunteering doesn't have to mean collecting funds with a tin can, cleaning bedpans, or passing out leaflets. Many modern charities, political groups, environmental groups, and the like are sophisticated organizations with interesting staffers and volunteers. You may be able to participate in anything from marketing communications to social events, at almost any level of involvement you choose.

53. Take a class.

Everyone suggests this; the options are
inexhaustible and the worst thing that
can happen is that you'll learn
something.

54. Teach something.

55. Go to class reunions.

56. Stop seeing people that you know
are bad for you.

This is for people who keep attracting
people who simply aren't sensitive, aren't
considerate, and *aren't going to change.*
Are you really so masochistic that you're
going to let yourself continually be
drawn to these bozos? If so, go for it.
Otherwise, *pass.* You know all the signs
by now, and every minute you waste is
time you could be with (or at least
looking for) someone who cares.

57. Go to Club Med; preserve the attitude.

Unless you have the looks of an iguana
and the personality of a stone, you will
meet people at Club Med. New friends
are virtually guaranteed, and your
probability of some sort of romance is
dramatically multiplied. Call *directly* and
be sure you choose a village for singles.
Why isn't it always this easy to meet
people? (P.S.—I am not in the pay
of Club Med.)

58. Talk to older people.

59. Talk to younger people.

60. Talk to couples.

61. Talk to neighbors.

62. *Leave the country.*

Foreigners in many places warmly welcome travelers. (Too bad we're not a little friendlier about it here.) You'll also be surprised to find Americans are suddenly friendlier when they're on foreign soil as well. Where have you always wanted to go? *Why not do it?* There are a million affordable plans. Schoolteachers have known about this for years. Push yourself as far as a travel agency and explore the idea. In particular, look into the new breed of "adventure travel" agents. Just be sure your agent has *actually been* to the destination you settle on, and isn't relying on little blurbs in a brochure.

63. Be positive.

64. Be realistic.

65. Be whimsical.

66. Be curious.

I mean with shop owners, students,
waiters, doctors, tourists, bartenders,
cabdrivers, hot-dog vendors, taxidermists,
salespeople, bell captains—everyone.
People are walking novels, with
fascinating facts, unusual places, and
interesting characters.

67. Investigate groups that attract singles (Sierra Club Singles, sports, social, etc.).

Groups, activities, and mixers *expressly* for meeting singles are often, ironically, the most awkward way of meeting people of all. They were almost excluded from the list, but for the exceedingly rare good ones and the assurances of some people that they've worked for them.

(Professional dating services were omitted. I've avoided suggestions that cost money and present about the same odds that you'd find in Las Vegas.) If you're going try singles groups, you'll increase your chances of a good time, and of meeting people, by selecting one that involves a sport, hobby, or cause that you like, rather than attending some meaningless bash. Plan to make friends rather than dates. Refer to #5; attend with a friend.

68. Attend civic meetings that affect you.

Oh, you talk a good game, but *are you
there* when they meet to discuss the
environmental risk of the new reactor
or the shortage of police in
your community?

69. Play volleyball
or other team or league sports.

It's great if you like fishing, but you're a
lot more likely to find a catch in coed
team sports, especially those that play
in tournaments or matches.

70. Talk to people in checkout lines,
movie lines, and elevators.

71. Make plans in advance.

72. Be spontaneous.

73. Visit a friend who lives in another city.

This is a sleeper. Even if your friend
lives someplace less dazzling than Saint-
Tropez, my theory is that you can have
fun in practically any city for three days.
With a friend, former classmate, even a
relative, you'll get free lodging and a
built-in circle of new friends. *You* can be
the occasion for your friend to plan a
party, picnic, or other gathering
of friends.

74. Join more groups that share your interests.

Duh. But are you *doing* it?

75. Get on the Net
(but don't be seduced by it).

Unfortunately, too many people get trapped on the Net, addicted to living out fantasies without leaving the security of their living rooms. But a "chat room" is no substitute for a real room, and your on-line virtual date may be a fourteen-year-old with an overactive imagination or a dirty old man. However, the Internet is also a genuine doorway to the real world. Some forms of conferencing can link you to people with mutual interests. Many services can inform and update you on activities or events near you. And in truth, it isn't completely unheard of for people who met in cyberspace to eventually wind up walking down the aisle.

76. If you're a man, learn the meaning
of an arabesque.

77. If you're a woman, learn the meaning
of a double reverse.

78. Quit that nasty habit.

79. Show up early.

81. Be in a play.

Act, paint sets, do publicity, greet people at the door, whatever.

82. Get your act together.

Maybe it's time to take a self-assessment
and make some home improvements. To
reexamine your career, your city, your
lifestyle, your assumptions. The author
of a recent column like mine wrote,
"If you want to have somebody,
be somebody." That doesn't mean you
have to be president. But are you the
best possible *you*?

83. Convert people you don't want to date into friends whenever possible.

So you're not in love. But as Rick said to Louie in *Casablanca,* "This could be the start of a beautiful friendship." Besides, why discard someone who could be part of an ever-expanding circle of friends that could lead to the person you're seeking?

84. See *When Harry Met Sally,*
and take a second look
at the Harrys and Sallys in your life.

When a good friendship turns into a
romance, it's a lot more likely to become
an enduring relationship than your fling
on the beach in Bora Bora.

85. Read *The 100 Best Ways to Stay Together.*

Many of the attributes that help keep
people together are of value from the
instant you meet. After all, that's the
moment when all relationships begin.
And for many people, that's also when
opportunities and difficulties with
communication and sensitivity
begin as well.

86. Silence your inner voices.

We aren't alone. Our brains are cluttered with voices waging an eternal internal debate. Should you approach him or her, or shouldn't you? Did they look your way, or didn't they? Will they notice it's a bad hair day, or that you forgot to shave, or that you're wearing your grubbies, or you feel a cold coming on or . . . *shuddduuup*! The person you want to meet or call isn't the person you're afraid of; it's you! *So shut up, move,* and remember #10.

87. *Persist.*

There are two ways to take that; both intended. First, don't let a rejection or two blow an evening, much less a weekend or longer. People are constantly being rejected and rejecting, and you've done it plenty of times yourself. Second, if you've found someone you really want to pursue, who has given you the brush-off, as one man who is now happily married to such a woman said, "That's when you learn what you're made of." This is not to suggest that you become the night stalker. Wait a few days, call again, and *keep it light.* Suggest lunch or brunch or a coffee or a hike instead of a heavy Saturday-night date. Get creative. I've met several happy couples who got their start because one was deaf to the word "no." One guy actually waited through a whole marriage for the woman he wanted. Extreme, yes, but . . . "Persistence pays," his wife says with a smile.

88. Eat at a sushi bar.

Okay, let's say you don't like sushi. You can always nibble something like California roll (crab, avocado, rice) or tempura. But I know few atmospheres as congenial. These places have none of the pressures of regular bars, and it's incredibly easy to strike up conversations.

89. Ski.

Admittedly, it's not available, affordable,
or desirable to everyone, but everything
from the lift lines to the lodges, pubs,
and hot tubs are conducive to meeting
people. Even if you're nowhere near
powder, there's probably a
ski club near you.

91. *Include* people.

It's always good form to introduce anyone with you and include them in the aura of your conversation (even if they're nonparticipants in the subject), rather than let them dangle next to you. When's the last time you said or heard someone say later, "Oh! I didn't realize you wanted to meet her!"

92. Look for lasting qualities
if you're looking for a lasting relationship.

Time is a thief; it dulls the brilliance of
her flashing blue eyes and the bulge of
his biceps. But it preserves qualities like
character and humor and honesty and
depth. It's easy to find a tennis partner;
it's a lot harder to find someone who
looks at life out of the same window.

93. *Blow up the TV.*

94. Go to church or temple.

I'm not particularly recommending that
you *pray* for the person of your dreams,
although it couldn't hurt. Fact is, if you
haven't been to church, temple, or other
religious institutions lately, you may find
they've changed. Many have expanded to
become centers for artistic, musical,
recreational, educational, cultural,
and social events.

95. *Return every smile.*

97. Let yourself be vulnerable
one more time.

98. *Don't wait for everything in your life to be perfect before going out.*

99. Treat every person as if they were
a conduit to new people, ideas, and magic.